Climbing the Rain

Also by Marvyne Jenoff

No Lingering Peace   poems
   Fredericton: Fiddlehead Press 1972

Hollandsong   poems
   Ottawa: Oberon Press 1975

The Orphan and the Stranger   poems
   Toronto: Wolsak and Wynn Publishers 1985

The Emperor's Body   re-invented folktales
   Victoria, BC: Ekstasis Editions 1995

Several chapbooks
   Toronto: Twoffish Press, 2006 to 2019
   www.marvynejenoff.org

Climbing the Rain

Marvyne Jenoff

Silver Bow
Publishing

Title: Climbing the Rain
Author: Marvyne Jenoff
Cover Photo: "Hush the Sibilant Rain" painting by Marvyne Jenoff
Layout and Design: Candice James
Editor: Candice James

All rights reserved including the right to reproduce or translate this book or any portions thereof, in any form without the permission of the publisher. Except for the use of short passages for review purposes, no part of this book may be reproduced, in part or in whole, or transmitted in any form or by any means, electronically or mechanically, including photocopying, recording, or any information or storage retrieval system without prior permission in writing from the publisher or a licence from the Canadian Copyright Collective Agency (Access Copyright).

www.silverbowpublishing.com
info@silverbowpublishing.com
© Silver Bow Publishing 2021
Silver Bow Publishing 720 Sixth Street, Unit # 5
New Westminster, BC V3L 3C5 CANADA

isbn: 9781774032039 book
isbn: 9781774032046 e book

Library and Archives Canada Cataloguing in Publication

Title: Climbing the rain / Marvyne Jenoff.
Names: Jenoff, Marvyne, author.
Description: Poems.
Identifiers: Canadiana (print) 20220166501 | Canadiana (ebook) 20220166536 | ISBN 9781774032039
   (softcover) | ISBN 9781774032046 (EPUB)
Classification: LCC PS8569.E57 C55 2022 | DDC C811/.54—dc23

Climbing the Rain

Rain falls,
from what beginning?

I rise,
toward what end?

Contents

Climbing the Rain ... 5

NOW

Sky Blue Umbrellas

A is for ... 15
It's There ... 16
Amethyst ... 18
Song without Nouns ... 20
January, Green ... 21
Work ... 23
October 2020, Walk to the Park ... 24
January 2021, Atonement ... 25
Mouse ... 26
My Genie ... 27
Five Friends Meet for Dinner on Eglinton East ... 28
Video Poem ... 30
About a Bed ... 31
Short Summer Night ... 32
Midsummer Gift of Waking ... 34
Sky Blue Umbrellas ... 36
Square Lullaby, Yonge and Eglinton ... 37

THEN

Embracing Union Station

Drum and Company ... 43
God Indoors ... 44
The Goose and the Commuter Train ... 45
Embracing Union Station ... 47
Bestiary ... 49
From Southern Ontario, A Sea Tale ... 51
Public Transit ... 52

Plain Truth ... 53
Letter Writer ... 54
A Lesson in Resuscitation ... 55
It Wishes ... 57
Ever 58

It's a Fish! It's a Plane!

Flying into Vancouver ... 61
Words Dream ... 62
Summer Story, Yonge and Eglinton ... 63
It's a Fish! It's a Plane! ... 65
Two Moons, Blue Table ... 66
QE II is the Ocean Liner ... 67
Choices ... 68
Little ... 69
Dinosaur Aloft ... 71
The Promised Hip ... 72

The Day She Never Saw the Weather

The Day She Never Saw the Weather ... 77
Order ... 79
Miracle near U. of T. ... 80
Ways of Mourning ... 83
Scattering ... 84
Ease ... 85
Water ... 86
You x 10 ... 88

NOW

Bone's Business

The Femur Breaks ... 95
Packing ... 96
Dream ... 98
Accepting Metal ... 99

Fish Tank ... 101
In Rehab ... 102
In the Night ... 103
Watching the Olympics ... 105
Zodiacs ... 107
The Missing Masculine ... 109
Birthday ... 110
Saving the Monkey ... 111
Wheeling ... 112
Still Healing ... 114
Leave-taking ... 115
Bones' Full Business ... 116

The Octave Difference in Our Voices

Hat, October ... 119
Selves ... 120
Risen ... 122
Singing ... 124
Sunday Morning ... 125
Potatoes ... 126
Not Seen nor Heard ... 128
High-Rise Living, Two Afternoons ... 129
Late Afternoon, My Place ... 130
Old Cotton Robe ... 131
Early March Birthday ... 132
Elder Sleepover ... 133

Dedications and Acknowledgements ... 135

Author Profile ... 139

NOW

Sky Blue Umbrellas

A is for

A is for what ails us
and for aimlessness,
the twins of aging.

Ailments assail us;
aimlessness can be achieved.

A is for anxiety when you're a child,
then it becomes angst,
now it's anxiety again.

Therefore aspire to aimlessness.
Encourage it on weekends,
free from medical appointments.

Imagine being airborne as long as you wish
alone in a silent, spacious airplane
without the airplane:
you've achieved aimlessness.

Make aimlessness the stronger twin.
From it arises articulateness,
amiability,
affection,
and
and

A is for *and*—
better than *end*.

It's There

Doctors know it's there, some artists, too:
that bump at the base of the thumb
with its little cheek.

Knitters discover it once we advance
to the four-needle knitting-in-the-round stage,
past socks, to gloves.

A firm ribbed cuff to warm the wrist
and then that tricky, satisfying part:
a fifth needle picks up stitches for a gusset;
each new row diagonally grows to protect
the jutting bone that branches sideways
like a winter tree.

The glove is easy to complete:
repeat in mirror image for its mate
and find another friend to knit for,
though it's not the friend's need
but the knitter's.

Glove after glorious glove she makes
for the sake of making them.
A series of self-portraits are they,
not ironic drawings
nor paintings preserving age after age,
but portraits that fond repetition spawns.

The Warmth Giver lives long
in the practice of her ancient art,
embraces new approaches;
unimagined yarns excite her mind,

while all we knitters come at last to this:

the odd stitch disappears,
through our astonished fingers the yarn slips,

thumbs falter and protest in pain.
To soothe it, doctors say,
use ice.

Amethyst

An elder nude, self-portrait:
Here I am in the studio, painting and being painted.
I recline in profile, left arm along the back of a low settee,
gaze fixed toward the amethyst bracelet on my wrist.

My painter self sees
right breast drooping sideways toward the hip,
old surgical scar persisting down the thigh,
striped towel, rose-patterned settee,
age-mottled arm sporting the amethyst bracelet.
I select from my candy-store of colours,
lay down large strokes.

The posing me is alternately nodding into naps
and fretting about my life outside the studio:
Left hand, committed to my cane,
means the right must always choose between
an umbrella and anything else at all;
and my thumb's not good—can't even knit,
my luscious yarns unused;
This alternate life, reclining into a painting, is much easier,
remembering too late my morning pills,
freed from deciding what to wear,
the bracelet permanently there—how nude is nude?

It's made of plastic, each bead stamped out the same,
but the light finds different angles through the facets;
varieties of amethyst excite the painting me,
elaborating details onto the canvas.
I stand back to see the larger work
and rest, unthinking, sit down with a cup of tea.

And the brush itself takes over, disregards
the stripes, the flowers as distractions from its purpose,
paints over them in layers. Settee eradicated

I appear to float, my flesh ghosts
into the background colour, shallow foam on sand.

My cloud of hair, approaching white,
contrasts across the painting with the amethyst bracelet.
Lifeline more precious than real gems it is,
its metal tag shadowed at my inner wrist
listing my medications,
what parts of me to treat with special care.

Which lurking danger will entrap me?
I could brave a few more seasons:
screw the ice grip back onto my cane;
into the rain or sun attempt an umbrella.

My back aches, so I know I'm here reclining,
my heft still flattening the towel,
right hand stroking the silky roses,
though by now I am invisible.
Up there on the canvas, where a sky could be,
remains the bracelet shaped as if around a wrist.

And so the plastic beads outlast me
and the colour amethyst, last thing I may see;
may it endure.

Song without Nouns

Just when we comfortably know it all
nouns leave us.

It would be nice to keep a few—forest, bird—
but no, whenever they please, nouns flee us,

leaving the *the's* bereft and stuttering,
preceded by *for's, with's* and *to's*
but going nowhere,
one-upping the *a's* and *an's*
now mootly.

Some nouns circle back unbidden,
say, the Abyss,
or worse, Eternity—
not even a *the*
nor we can cling to it,

we who once asked
where all the flowers had gone.

January, Green

Nothing hurts, and the January sun
lifts up this elder heart with a picnic feeling:
I'm bringing sandwiches to you as you recover.

>Same feeling as summer with my other, long-dead friend
>when 10-year-olds could take a streetcar to the park.
>In our pockets besides children's tickets
>there would be coins, perhaps a dollar bill.
>Matching pink tin lunch pails at our sides,
>we walked primly from the bus stop onto a green meadow,
>as we called it, with a No Picnicking sign.

>Moral discussion, then giggling as we sat behind the sign,
>getting away with something,
>opening the neat, waxed paper,
>shared in halves the egg and tuna sandwiches
>our mothers made us on sliced bread.
>They'd sent us off with blessings,
>likely some cookies, too, back then.

Today in January on the subway, still that picnic feeling,
a wrap and a focaccia in a take-out bag.
As your station nears—not enough hands, the train in motion—
I sort out my gloves, hat, earmuffs,
zip up my impractical new coat,
maneuver my over-the-shoulder bag around the hood,
grasp the lunch bag and my cane,

And up the escalator into the cold sunshine,
still that picnic feeling.
You meet me at the door; your knee really feels much better.
You are able to take my heavy coat,
unpack our lunch, get plates, make tea.

We sit down to our two half-sandwiches,

discuss their contents—chicken, humus—small talk.
Then silently, like saying grace,
we bask in our well-being, and we know
there will be green again.

Work

I finally agree to work with you again.
You email three thumbs up,
    deep yellow icons.
I reply I am impressed,
having only two thumbs, arthritic at that.

You add a fourth.
We start to plan.

Age falls away,
my back muscles reclaim
their long-forgotten forward thrust,
spine flexes once-hunched shoulders
back to square.

A two-edged portent,
all those thumbs up,
    caution-coloured.
But I face the screen in old pyjamas,
chest wide, lungs ready to accept
whatever's out there.

October 2020, Walk to the Park

Down the windy street a flimsy mask flew,
brushed past mine.
Is that a kiss these days?

Must be from those dear nonchalants ahead,
thin-legged, racing against each other.
I am cane-paced, slow but steady.

It blew right past me, meant to keep going.
I wouldn't want anyone else's mask.
I wouldn't want anyone else's legs.

Even anyone's who'd bound up the subway steps
two at a time, I've even seen three,
back when the subway sped us on.

It's not a race, though all of us are in it.
There they are already in the park, sparring, dancing;
now I do that with words.

What they're doing would free any mask.
With all those legs, let them be horses and escape
the mask-denier's end.

My own legs slow, my breath too, I could stop awhile
and listen past the next street's traffic
to the hush of wind-blown leaves.

No race, but there's a finish. Mine could be
this triumph: stand tall and still and let the leaves
fete me with their colours, passing kisses,

spin a cape of scintillation round me
till their murmur lessened.
Then the silent mask of snow.

January 2021, Atonement

Down the windy tree-lined street my flimsy mask blew off:
my fault, I wore it under my nose,
protecting no one.

As the wind propelled me home to get another mask
a hat flew past me,
old woman's hat, gnarled flowers

and a child's doll flew past
then the doll house
then one of those fat plastic tricycles

Safely up the elevator to my unit
—mad winds out there, and purple clouds—
I searched not for another flimsy mask
but the means to make a proper one:
tight-woven fabric from an extra pillowcase
and a filter: tissue, dryer sheet?

I like to make things. As I was peacefully sewing
enough masks to save everyone in my building
a branch flew up to my 12th-floor window and crashed through,
a rat sprang out from among the glass-torn leaves

But I am safely in the other room embroidering the masks
with stiff but pretty cross-stitch flowers no wind would ever covet.
Ten masks a day I'll make
till everyone on my street is rescued, even their dogs

and I, too, am saved, forgiven,
nay, heroic.

Mouse

A man fears a mouse
and the mouse, fear in its very beating,
dreams of running.

The man aspires to mountains, has a plan:
deftly he masters numbers,
with their science and currency
creates proliferating edifices
not quite as high as mountains
but they're well built and they're his.

He circles home to his proud penthouse,
where he lies with a woman larger than himself,
not quite fearing
the mouse-beat of her heart.

Smallness infiltrates his sleep
and pivots from the mouse
to smaller creatures: spiders, bedbugs,
and the unseen things he knows live on his skin

And even tinier ones he's heard exist,
with ugly names in other languages.
His numbers stumble at their smallness
and how fast they propagate,
vast progeny swarm toward his head.

On a vast field he races with the mouse and loses,
vanishes in the vortex of a rabbit-hole, still running

till touch wakes him,
saves him from this foolish dream.
Touch the warm woman.
Touch the solid wall.

My Genie

Invisible as the virus is my genie
though I know it's with me;
it finds me pretty flowered masks
and grows and grows my hair

And, for this indoor life it's taught me Zoom:
now I can sort of visit you and you
and even you in Timbuktu,
compare our hair and earrings on the screen

It's taught me online shopping,
how in one breath to browse and buy
said earrings, kitchen gadgets, fancy sheets
and this preposterous bedside lamp:

No shade, no light bulb,
but a flat white stem arising from an angled base—
here's where my kind of genie lives.
Bright, brighter, brightest,

One playful touch can light it,
charge my phone,
start coffee in the morning,
text you and you that I'm awake and well

One more touch, and colours flower in the base,
pulsing and pulsing through their rainbow—
that's my genie fending off the virus.
I am charmed.

Five Friends meet for Dinner on Eglinton East

I let them pass me, all those people
released from the subway rushing home.
I prefer to stroll the half-mile to the restaurant,
stretching out like a ceremony the anticipation
of meeting there.

Strolling is the pace for me.
To my left beyond mesh barriers
loom all manner of construction vehicles
working hard on ever more finishing touches
for the Crosstown subway line.

Comfortable walking in my better shoes
I deftly navigate the chopped-up sidewalk
Do I need this cane at all?
To my right, the little views down cross-streets,
light-faceted glimpse of gridded condos
and a few young trees bright in the touch of sun.

Then the last traffic light before the restaurant.
I arrive third, safely in the middle,
We greet, I sit and set aside
my hat, sunglasses, mask.

....

It's dark, leaving together for the subway,
we stand up and stretch our legs,
and in the pleasure of a full-paced walk
those four stride across the street as the green light ends
and I stand waiting for the next one.

They wait for me to cross, then walk ahead again.
Yet they keep looking back, and one by one
come back to walk with me,
and catch up to the others stopped at a traffic light
or window of a different restaurant

where we all agree to meet another time.
And so it's *we* again,
five friends into the subway.

Video Poem

Lazy summer I could make a video
let the world know all
my Mr. Loose-End-Type Disappointments

One of them said make a whole video of me
I certainly could and he wouldn't like it, but I said
I don't know about that
thinking up this poem instead

I said come to the park
he said I don't know about that
thinking of his life
so we planned to go

Long ago we disregarded clothes once even in a park
but now just on my head I juggle
hearing aids the better to hear you with
glasses with those big sunglasses on top to foil old age
hat with chin cord so we needn't chase after it

Shoes a quandary
sandals a trip hazard
broken bones could be another video
do I want glamour or my everyday sneakers
that mean pants not a dress
I never do decide

We're floating barefoot just above the grass
perhaps we do the circuit round the park
small park just down the street
while I pretend it's the larger park a drive away
with a stream and little creatures on the rocks
perhaps we do a few circuits building up talk

and at my door he says for the first time
I'm sorry or goodbye.
That's what I wanted.
No video now.

About a Bed

Is lying flat no longer for the living?
My new bed adjusts:

Top part rises up like a sideways book,
bottom rises up to close that book.

Royalty at last, I rule by thumb:
one touch on the remote
relaxes both parts to my comfort,
one more touch commands a purple glow,
faint carpet in the dark,
lest I should trip

Could I really sleep in this position
surely meant for reading, writing,
watching television,
napping while watching television?

New-fangled surface stuff
cocoons me
what metamorphosis awaits the aged?

I slip into television napping mode
held as in a little boat
moored and slightly bobbing on the water

I could just wait here, drift into sleep,
but the oars
—a book, a pen—
seek out my hands.
I row.

Short Summer Night

The blackout curtains help:
as long as I believe it's night I sleep,
my high-rise modest and too far from trees
to blame my waking on the pre-dawn
din of birds I've heard about.

Even in heat leftover from the day
I fervently believe it's night, embrace my sleep
but whatever wakes the birds slips past
my ineffectual hallway fan.

One hand still clutching sleep,
the other, self-directed,
folds aside the bunched-up top sheet,
twists my nightie off and tosses it onto the far chair.
I'm grunt-pleased with my aim.

The first hand curls me back toward sleep,
the second flings me over, splays me out,
inviting any waft of air,
my ribs a wide page ready for print.

What wakes the birds discovers me,
I twitch aware in the curtained darkness
pinioned by the unseen sun's demand:
Experience this day.

Surely a gift but still, eyes closed,
I cling to the prior gift:
dilemma of my dark half-waking floods my mind
with coolness of imagined trees,
melodious back and forth of birds, of words
into that known-in-the-bone soft opening of the sky,
blue morning glories in my childhood garden

and so secret in the dark my life's recurring wonder
even in my 77th (double lucky) summer:
What shall I be when I grow up?

Midsummer Gift of Waking

On my right side I wake,
my first awareness:
comfort of the cotton t-shirt
draped over my eyes for proper darkness.

Pretty t-shirt, gathered at the v-neck point;
loose thread still there
from when I fixed it,
wore it for our first time at the park,
and you remember it.

I slide it off and
lo, there be light
around the black-out shade,
but not bright sunlight—
rain? cloud? just very early?

Curiosity turns me on my back
and I squint to read the digits on the TV box—
six o'clock, or eight?
Once I got up at five and nothing happened.

On my left side now and no discomfort
but the arm connected
to that shoulder business.

Then sideways up,
legs swinging childlike
over the side of the high bed
as I sit awhile averting
vertigo of sudden standing,
contemplate first choices for the morning:

Get to the laundry room before anyone else,
or breakfast first,

and oatmeal or rye toast and cheese,
and at the table or perched at the window
watching the rain or cloud or light progress:

the gift of choices,
gift of day.

Sky Blue Umbrellas

Late summer day, my subway train
speeds toward our timeless afternoon.

We greet and, cane assisted, make our way.
You have new dangle earrings.

Delicate wristwatches we wear, and scarves,
I in a flowered one to foil the season's turning,
you, the scholar, in a print that might be
ancient symbols.

Here we are lunching on the fenced back patio.
Flowers and trees protect us from the city,
not-so-ancient city noisily borne ahead
by the news of the world.

Out here where no TV insists upon the present
we analyze Victoria, Guinevere, Cleopatra,
the coloured gossip-filled balloons rising above
sky blue umbrellas with their flimsy shade
and dissipating up to where we in another time
may meet them.

Meanwhile we, the source, the ballast, pay our bills,
rise carefully from the table
scarves flamboyant in the breeze lead us elsewhere
for still more tea,
perhaps dessert.

Square Lullaby, Yonge and Eglinton

Upon the expanse of graveled roof
a little garden in a square of bricks,
shape shadowed by the lushly watered greens;
the haze of daisies and their August friends
bloom full in their semi-season.

Chocolate has no season;
chosen, daily, from the mall across the street,
then home to an indoor pleasure, where the quiet
enhances whispers of the wrapper
and the savouring of the little squares one by one
or two by two into the evening.

Large square roof to see the sunset from,
and south beyond the nurturing mall
the intersection marked by zebra crossings.
Once they were square, now skewed long-term
while the bright new subway line goes in,
done any day now.

North, encroaching just in spitting distance,
giant square tower already higher than this roof
grows one floor weekly, concrete-walled:
May the dusk obscure it!

Dusk that soothes the humming city
and surrounds more quietly this roof,
where now the hushing flowers darken
to a square of fragrance.

Little square garden,
square-tiled path over the gravel,
square window in the door,
last square of chocolate,

squarish room,
squarish bed,
and so to sleep.

THEN

Embracing Union Station

Drum and Company

My friend my friend my
drummerfriend wakes
from his books and his pens,

and his hands his hands his
fingers call him to the drum to the
drum making paperlace patterns for
the tummy of the drum

His head his laugh his
head winds high and his ankles
flex and his toes awake to the rhythm of the
loud hand the sharp hand the
belly of the bellydrum that spins
in a concentrated dance, a dance

that flies, that flies, that springs from the
clay and the cords and the skin of the bumdrum,
dance of the monolithic thigh bone,
dance of the rise of the drum and the
drummer to the rise of the
drummerbird.

I am done I am spun I have
bellied to the memory of the drum
soft on the toes of the toes of a

kiss where I listen for the end
of the end of the drumming and my
listening for the drummerwas the
drummerwas my friendagain,
my friendagain,
my friend.

God Indoors

Where my darling sleeps,
where he has lain down in faith and now
utterly sleeps,
and the covers soft on his body roll
like the sea
and grow calm;

where his hair flows back on the pillow,
baring his impassive ear
and swell of his jaw,
where all the little points of beard pierce tinily
the slow, salt warmth of sleep,

God hovers,
whole above stillness,
then through the first flicker of smile
slips into his heart and curls there,

    until to a startled eye
a God-hurled beam announces corners, doors,
white light

    until a smile awakens
and a rainbow arc furls flowers onto the wall,
sea-patient leaves, yea, softly,
even the pink
shadows of leaves.

The Goose and the Commuter Train

I guess this makes me
the girl out here in Mississauga
with the brown umbrella,
now that the girl in Toronto with the green umbrella
lent hers to you yesterday
for your journey back out to Mississauga.

This morning, on your way to Toronto
        to return her green umbrella
you take along my brown one
in case it should rain on your way back here
        to Mississauga.

All we need now is a girl in Toronto with a blue umbrella
to complete the classic situation
of the man on the two-seater raft:

he had to cross the river first with the goose and
        leave it on the other side,
        then come back
and take the buckwheat over,
        leave it on the other side
        and come back with the goose,
then take the fox over
        and leave it with the buckwheat,
and finally come back again for the goose,
if he wanted to end up on the other side
with all the eyes intact.

Still, I want you to feel free to borrow
my brown umbrella any time.
Everyone knows we were childhood friends,
and I wouldn't want you to be seen
with cloud on your face.

I also have an orange and white umbrella
with blossoms in an Asian manner,
zebras, anemones,
fish that utter dreams.

You glimpsed it once.
You may think that's the one you have right now
tucked under your arm so its wings
won't flap on the train.
But I want you to know
the things I give you to take away to Toronto—
my keys, my past—
are spare.

Embracing Union Station

Triumphant,
and a little sad,
and standing on my toe,
he reaches the station rafters and looks
down on the tops of trains,
considering destinations.

Considering trains this toe will never enter
he does not forget me,
lowers his hand
      (kind butterfly)
around my hair
      (no more).

He is standing on my toe,
and the nail splits, O,
and the red pain straight as a whistle claims
my heart, my wobbling heart,
dear bubbling frog of a heart grows
wary, joyful, still, resourceful,

sprouts a nail,
and the heart nail
splits and the bright pain
quickens the question he's fostered inside me,
a monster who'd burst
who'd be born
and beat him
and cry

Silenced by insinuating kisses and quick visits,
how can I know you'd love on my amazing sheets
an agile but complaining woman?

The trapped pain festers, and my toe knows

he is standing on my toe,
and the bone splits, O,
and seeping and hissing at last onto the platform
my blood curses thus:
This man is sinister, loved, dangerous, strong.

He flings away my arms.
He wants that train.

One nail,
one miserable nail—
I thought you'd promised
total crucifixion.

Bestiary

1. The Fishes

Here's where we learn the colours
blue, cold, depth
and darkness

Decisions here are quick,
flick of the tail
and cold

Nothing looks back,
our neckless water-bodies
streamlined to one direction

So easily I slip beside you
and in sleep
so easily beyond

2. Or Like Birds

Birds court, they say,
and are faithful

Your despair illuminates you
with bright plumage.
It is your means of soaring,
means of sorrow

You court me with a plea,
Help me, you say;
if I pluck out your sorrow
where would your wings be?

Help me, you say,

you court me with a plea,
would have me make a cloak,
a cap of you
and wear it.

3. Mammals' End

This is the end of us,
one taste of breast and hair
and we crave forever
wine and bread

And a shared table,
house so big,
the smells of children round us,
contact sports.

Apart,
our unrequited smells turn rancid
and the hair, sparse;
a naked stance, ridiculous;
the sheets, polyester.

From Southern Ontario: A Sea Tale

An urban woman and a maritime man
went for a walk by the lake
as a parting gesture,

his steel trunks all packed and she
already flighty with appointments
so as not to be lonely.

She busied herself in the gravel,
poking and rummaging like a bird,
and settled,
as he waited softly,
on a piece of granite
coloured to match her newly upholstered
chairs. She could also see it

scrubbed and pretty on a bathroom shelf
or, as she shifted its weight, a natural foil
for a green plant.

And as he ran heavily along the shore,
bearing his defeated kindnesses
and the whole bleak gamut of their seasons,

she mistook his harsh winter-grimace
for acceptance, and she thought
when she missed him she could
hold the stone to her ear.

He slows now, breathing large over
the shore for him endless and the horizon far,
his generous love recalled in colours shrunken
hard and small, his generous
sorrow seeking whales.

Public Transit

There you are, settled in a window seat,
face in a guilt of scentless flowers,
your smile re-living times with me—

your skin begins to tingle
like the spider
on my windowsill—

and by the time you see me standing there
you're blushing.
You've never seen me in a winter coat.
I look my age.

Balancing my life's possessions on my head—
briefcase of negligees,
two caged white cockatiels
and cabbages in newspaper
from your hometown—

I could sit on the flowers and greet you,
I could become your neighbour,
laugh or cry,

but I pass by
and find a window on the other side.

Still, there is the smell of fish,
inside the newspaper a photo you'd forgotten,
taken when you were fat.

Plain Truth

Mysteries, he said,
you make mysteries, he said,
you make mysteries where there are none:

That's what's wrong with you.

Letter Writer

He doesn't say what he's asking for,
he sends a summary with no conclusion
lest it be stolen,
he doesn't sign his name

If only some prominent person
would just learn the language
he has had to invent
to express himself.

A Lesson in Resuscitation

    I did not expect her face to be blue.

She whispered from her bed, *It's nothing. But this morning I was dead for a moment. I had an awful pain, then nothing. Someone shouted, "Breathe, breathe!" and I think I heard a prayer—who am I to question? The police came, and an ambulance, and here I am, back again!*

My dear, don't be so shocked. At my age you expect such things. Now, come closer and tell me how you are.

She lay back and closed her eyes. Her face was still pretty blue.

    I whispered in her ear, *There's a man in my life.*

Ooh! Marvelous! she said. *Tell me more.*

    Well, we met...

How exciting! How very exciting! She sat up. *See what you are doing to me with your enthusiasm! Go on.*

    Well, he says...

That sound's wonderful, my dear! You know my philosophy—if you can talk to each other before <u>and</u> after, then you know it's love.
    But, she said, tapping off the top of a boiled egg and looking inside, *if you want my advice—I'm giving it to you anyway—I think you are spending too much time waiting. The best thing in your situation is to have <u>two</u> men.*
    My dear, don't be so shocked. Find a second man now, while you are feeling so...so...energetic.
    You know, dear, in all the excitement this morning there was such a nice young policeman! What a pity he didn't take off his clothes. He reminded me of a delightful man I once knew in Vienna...

    I knew a man in Winnipeg, I said,
and she said, *Paris*
    I said, *Parry Sound*
she said, *The Riviera*
    I said, *Rainy River*
she said, *San Francisco*
    and I asked, *Are you sure it's okay for you to laugh so much?*
and she said, *Nobody forbids me to laugh! San Francisco!*
    so I said, *Saskatoon*
she said, *Hong Kong*
    I said, *Flin Flon.*

As we sat by the window having tea
we looked out over the city lights and agreed upon Toronto,
    just in time for me to catch the last train back to Mississauga.

Her hair was red again right down to the roots.
At the door she kissed both my cheeks and said,

My dear, you look marvelous,
absolutely marvelous!
You know, the way you rushed in
I was sure you had <u>bad</u> news.

It Wishes

It wishes to happen,
it hovers aloft,
how lusty and soft,
now soaring, now flitting

it wishes, it winks,
how wisely it tingles
o'er wrinkles and hair,
it hums everywhere

it widens with weather
it narrows with wit
it tingles with wishing,
O wild, wondrous it

how nicely it whistles
how sweetly it nestles
O happily happen,
O happen to me.

Ever

Whether lover
whether other
whether either
neither knows

how the nose discovers feather
how the lips discover leisure
love can rival thorn and rose
rival how the weather blows

whether either, whether neither,
winter hovers into spring
summer's coming any ever
summer lovers everything.

It's a Fish! It's a Plane!

Flying into Vancouver

Mountains are higher than hotels,
hotels are higher than trees.

Mountains are older than trees,
trees are older than me,
I am older than the hotel.

Hotels are built to forget,
but trees remember.
(Was my birth year good for you,
with a nice, thick growth ring?)

The mountains sit there,
shedding snow.
Down below the water doodles,
prattles, saying nothing.

Trees enter my lone room.
We thrive, we tangle.

Words Dream

Words dream of puzzles
where they flit
not fit
among the squares

They dream of leaping
and the little squares
fade and sleep
and dream of colour

Summer Story, Yonge and Eglinton

If I didn't have to bite this bullet
I'd live a hundred years.
If I didn't have to live a hundred years
I'd eat lots of ice-cream right now.

If I didn't have to read this book
I'd get another book, not bullet,
from the library.
The eager check-out queue would wind
upstairs, down, around the block,
so many readers waiting,
I'd become a novelist,
there's still time.

If I didn't have to stand in this queue,
I'd crouch down to shoe level and surmise
who hikes,
who strolls in shopping malls and eats ice-cream,
who anchors, with which foot,
their reading-writing-rocking chair.

If I didn't have to sit in this chair and rock, I'd walk
down to the lake and out onto the water,

And walking to the island I'd espy
a prince on a white sailboat,
who has to rescue an innocent princess
but encounters me.

I'd consider being rescued,
for we all,
even the rescued,
still want rescuing.

We'd find he has an anchor,
and we'd talk, and I'd be
Lucy Relaxo,
Joan of Arts

And if I weren't so busy living a hundred years
we'd stroll on the island of no bullets ever,
mock duck calls,
sail into the endless summer sunset.

If it didn't have to be summer
there would be
no prince, no queue, no story.

It's a Fish! It's a Plane!

You call this a bookstore
and you don't serve fish?

Shelves full of vegetable colours
and you don't serve fish?

Airplanes are shaped like fish
but they don't wiggle.
Their wings are stiff,
and not as soft as pretty-feathered wings
of chickens.

Once they served me chicken on a plane.
They don't do that anymore.
I'm done with travelling.

That fish-shaped thing
up there descending toward the airport,
silver wrapped with coloured stripes and logo,
may well be chocolate

but that would be dessert.
Here I am in the bookstore
waiting for fish.

Two Moons, Blue Table

Two moons on a blue table.
Big One squats
like the heaviest melon ever;
it could win that prize.

Little One skitters round it,
teasing, skirting the table's edge,
would sing and chatter if it could.

Big One imposes,
lest you dare approach.
Little One, dimpled,
merrily bounces off it.

Open the window for them,
tactfully nudge Big One out
into its rightful orbit,
stately or cumbersome,
depends who's watching.

Little One already bouncing at and out
the window, door or chimney,
heckling in farewell,
seeking the widest orbit ever.

QE II is the Ocean Liner

Dear Queen Elizabeth,
Your Majesty,
I found a pencil sharpener
that belongs to you
with E II R and a little crown
stamped on it.

I picked it out from the ones not yours,
stamped QE II
(how clever of me to know the difference),
in the lost-and-found
of the Toronto Reference Library,
not the library of the QE II,
where, I understand, they give out
pencil sharpeners
rather than baseball caps or magnets.

Dear Magnate Queen,
I want you to know how happy I am to have
from among all the riches in the world
this pencil sharpener,
which I'd also be happy to return to you
if you'd only say the word.

Then I'd have a word from you
or else this pencil sharpener stamped E II R
under a little crown,
either way, one step a little closer
to the riches of the world.

Choices

TV Detective X in the rainy dark
single-handedly solves a 50-year-old train robbery
and catches a most-wanted serial killer at the same time:

__a) All detectives catch serial killers
__b) All serial killers get caught
__c) No other serial killers get caught
__d) No one but TV Detective X catches serial killers.

TV Heiress Y in the glow of Old-World antiques
single-handedly raises billions for a new opera,
rescues a child and finds true love forever:

__a) All heiresses find true love forever
__b) True love forever is always found
__c) True love forever is never found
__d) No one but TV Heiress Y finds true love forever.

Poet M, on a shaded afternoon,
amid stale bed-pillows, cheap chocolates and neglected cats,
watches TV instead of writing poetry:

__a) All poets watch TV instead of writing poetry
__b) All possible poetry gets written
__c) No poetry gets written
__d) No one but Poet M watches TV instead of writing poetry

__e) Some poets watch TV sometimes and write poetry sometimes.

Poet M, remote in one hand, pencil in the other,
writes a poem about TV.

Little

The little waves in the swimming pool
know neither surf nor sea,
know only you and me and the indoor swimming pool,
its vaulted windows, sky and trees reflected piecemeal
in the little waves that rise and play directions

lapping at me and you and you,
our new deep coloured swimsuits green, dark blue,
lap and turn to coloured ripples multiplying
you and you and me and Green and Blue and Flower
exercising in the gently purling waves

oh, little is as little does,
the ripples at the spandex glints of swimsuits,
colourful against them turn them for a moment sleek,
our bodies sleek as we bob in the deep end
tingling, singing virtue when we've just begun

The virtuous waves of the swimming pool
are not so faithful as they seem,
knowing no place where waves can truly swell,
confined, nevertheless in their own way true and full,
making a place of perpetual littleness
where the waves repeat and are new

and you and I, and you and you and I repeat,
adding now and then a little twist,
another twist, a stretch, another stretch, and then we leave behind,
not far behind,
our littleness,
and comet-tailed with droplets we vault up and out onto the deck,

our sudden human weight a moment on the cool-tiled deck,
pausing before the larger world
columned by living trees

our cedar-slatted building with all its vaulted glass nevertheless

solid, monumental as the moment of beginning foam
on breakers,
we break free to surf the skies.

Dinosaur Aloft *(at the Royal Ontario Museum)*

How sleep loves bones:
nightly she tends Tyrannosaurus,
comforts through the thundering seasons of its life
and in its death holds deep its darkening bones.

Discovery, slow dynamite, brings into light those bones
and Latin-names them, leaches them of data,
resurrects them into this skeleton above us balanced,
skull posed downward toward a whiff of prey.

Parched spaces pattern the dark bones
exposed against the white geometry of windows,
where stark light through years of afternoons
would bleach them.
Is this the end, the static heaven of a sunny day?

Or does the huge head nod?
Is this instead a solstice, one attenuated day
which sleep now coaxes toward an eon of descent?
Is there a greater cycle bearing us round,
bones, data and discoverers, into another dark
where sleep and love are one?

The Promised Hip *(reflections before surgery)*

1.

Replacing pain with light,
the surgeon's promise.

Where the old hip was,
gladness will tentatively venture
through my net of nerves,

new light,
unseen but felt,
like an inner day.

2.

Day fades,
all light succumbs to sleep.
In dreams I seek old habits:

left hand reaches for the cane
it fears to shed;

right hand, end
of its neck-pinched nerve,
clutches a pencil
it vows to keep.

3.

The Cane and Pencil,
haven for hobblers and scribblers,

those of us who remember
wood and paper,

reared on the intricate
nerve tracery
of words hand-written.

4.

Titanium: the word, handwritten,
is itself an earring,
tinkly with dotted i's,

yet, Titan-strong,
it also makes a hip

to tingle in the dark of me,
its texture itching to embrace
new-growing bone.

5.

Replace, embrace—
what lies ahead?
Dared pleasure of a simple balanced step,

What flies ahead?
Daft dream of cartwheels scattering sunlight,

but first,
but now,
how morning lights the surgeon's halo!
Here we go.

The Day She Never Saw the Weather

The Day She Never Saw the Weather

That day, she never saw the weather,
nor heard her husband say
I've left your eggs in the frying pan.
Don't forget to feed your animals.

She pulled on one sock under her nightgown
and, looking for the other,
nibbled a handful of spaghetti from the fridge.

That day, she never saw the weather
friendly at the window, for, inside,
the house they were paying off was far
too large and cold,
and she was twenty-five years old,

and looking for the other sock,
chewed one my one (and didn't read the label)
a handful of pills,

felt at her ankle
Dog's and Cat's mealtime affection,
so they all went into the closet to find
Teddy Bear (she was saving him all this time)
and the one-eyed doll and blankets,

packed an egg-and-spaghetti picnic
in the wastebasket,
remembered the ketchup.

She gathered them all into the little yellow
Rabbit in the garage,
whatever the weather,
started the motor,

and they all

brightly
softly
fell
down.

Order

Father stayed in the coal mine,
Mother stayed in the well,
I have no home, no womb, no pain,
no song: I count and spell.

Miracle near U of T
*(Women's Writing Collective Poetry Experience,
Hart House, University of Toronto, May 1977)*

At first, I felt right at home,
with women congratulating one another
for being liberated.

Surely that's why I'd been invited:
I was the most liberated of all,
having transcended the need for
spices, warm winter clothing, health insurance
and poetry readings,
but nobody congratulated me.

So when one of the women wrote poems against men,
I objected: that wasn't polite.
If I were the sort of person who went in for friends
I'd certainly be kind enough
to include some of our male counterparts.

One woman read about having two mother tongues
and a different personality in each.
I went on about how lucky I'd been:
My parents didn't talk to me, so I have no personality.
I got a good Winnipeg education—
English, math, music—interesting activities
and no need for psychiatrists.

Other women read poems about marriage, separation,
children, childlessness, humiliation. Sad poems.
Others read about beauty, aging, freedom, the sea.
All clichés to me, the Truly Liberated.
When my turn came
I read a poem about statistics.

Then, just as I was about to leave,

a distinguished poet whose name I'd always feared
approached me and said,

*I remember a poem of yours
that appeared twenty-seven years ago in Vogue,
and I wanted to tell you
that your use of a comma in the last line
was brilliant!*

I was touched.
I found myself moving from one group to another
bestowing opinions.
I stayed to the end.

And I felt so magnanimous
walking toward the subway
with a cheque in my pocket for appearing near U of T,
that I couldn't wait to get home to write more poems.

It was such a beautiful May evening,
with fresh-cut grass
and trees in bloom,
that I thought I might even write
sexy poems.

And then, as I crossed north on Hoskin Avenue,
a miracle:
a branch of Manitoba maple appeared
right in the middle of the pavement.
As I ran toward it, I tripped and skinned my knee.
In the wound I felt real Winnipeg gravel.
The fragrance of cabbage rolls filled the air over Queen's Park,
thinning the traffic and scattering the would-be lovers.
Only the squirrels were left,
and a little north-end-Winnipeg-type house,
not the kind we lived in, but a modest one
that we might have been able to afford,

and I ran right in
slammin' the screen door and hollerin' out
Hey, Ma! Hey, Pa
Remember me?

Ways of Mourning

Through laundry:

She stuffs too much into the washer,
lets it over-dry,
looks rumpled wherever she goes
because her mother, decades dead,
would sort her clothes and iron them,
even the easy-care fabrics.

Through money:

He uses a seat-of-the-pants method
of budgeting, non-budgeting,
just fine for now but no thought for the future
because his absent father
dealt so well with such things.

Through disability:

I could affect a cane, confine myself to home,
knitting, TV; a cat would clinch it,
because my first love and I,
or a different love and I,
or I and a different he or he or he
at every intersection in this city
used to talk, then kiss, then quarrel
and keep walking for a while.

Through decor:

On the shelves because they once were trees,
near the books because they once were trees,
arrange wheel-thrown ceramic vessels,
leave them empty: no little indoor plants,
no greenhouse flowers.

Scattering

Days since your death
and I'm still calling others by your name.

Friends, yes, and also servers
where we used to meet for lunches years ago,
and other restaurant patrons. And bus drivers
on routes to the well-treed neighbourhoods
we used to walk in. Passengers, too,
even on the subway; polite ones say
Sorry, that's not my name.

Perhaps there's something in my voice
that causes them to really listen, and go home
and say
and log onto the internet
(caught up with you at last)
and say,
someone strangely called me by this name today.
Have you heard of her?

Soon there's a world of people
wishing they'd known you.

And what of you, yourself, up there
freed from your failing body?
Do you know your name is spoken and relayed by others,
stretched to a wind-borne sound?

Fitting how far your thinning name has reached,
but here, back home, no solid speaking presence.
Now we will never be able to agree:
what was the massive object
that poor squirrel was trying to carry up a tree?
And did it get where it was going?

Ease

What made my sudden voice
so loud in that quiet space
just yesterday as we four lingered over tea?

Perhaps the sun through window blinds
across the softness of the tablecloth, so white,
recalled in me the light so long ago

across that spartan office,
shared scene of betrayal,
blame against me over time,
my only solace looking through the window,
trees offering their seasons.

Yesterday we were spinning out
mild conversation for its pleasant sake.
What then, made me cry out
as if to the portraits watching from the walls.
blurting from that deep buried time
impossible to summarize?

Perhaps you three are wondering, concerned.
But I'd prefer, because we are not close,
the delicacy of your unconcern,

stumbling as you did as if upon a sudden room
and my forced false confession,
as of you caught me braying,
praying.

Water

No desert is our life of shopping, browsing,
lunching well-dressed upon the patio with friends.
Art is our water.

In museums we support we see
a desert through the irony of watercolour,
which makes the desert shimmer and recede,

And loosens mountains as they loom,
the very mountains we have climbed for winter getaways,
real, rough-flanked mountains from whose peaks
we've watched the distant ocean flatten.

Watercolour oceans, fierce with battling ships,
are fun to paint, the books say, spatter the whiteness,
thumb against the brush, for spray.
Snow is fun, too: wet the white paper,
flow in pale shapes and call them shadows.

When the real snow goes
and turns our homes to summer
we return to lie on quiet water
—lake or swimming pool, no matter—
liquid of a long-accustomed lover's touch,

and just below us little fish-shapes flit
into the vessel of our minds—we can make art, too—
a liquid image of odd flotsam,
prowling fish with rows of teeth,
appropriately pricks us with trepidation.

Art, like water, keeps our life-oasis safe
from the imagined (dare to look closely)
desert which surrounds us,
undeniable desert parched with strife.

In the shade of the museum
once again upon the patio we lunch, agree
how blessed we are by art, our own diversion
as summer is from winter,
peace from war.

You x 10

You (#1), my fellow early riser, meet me for breakfast
where they serve a little square of chocolate after every meal.
We are cleverly in time to get our accustomed table,
and You (#2), our waitress, remember what we like.
Our laughter-lengthened visit strengthens me
for lunch with You (#3).

You (#3) were elected and I lost. Our lunch is brief.
I operate on empty: Sometimes I think I go for long walks.
Sometimes I think crossing the street to buy chocolate is a walk.
I do the laundry, grunt of satisfaction; cook soup that looks okay,
but suddenly I see how I can re-arrange the kitchen cupboards
and I'm my old self again.

I gather papers for the evening's meeting,
arrive before the rush for coffee and cookies
and chat a bit with You (#3, yes) and You (#4)
before sitting as usual at the far edge of the room.
You (#5) come all the way over and sit beside me, and I soften,
and You (#6) are visibly disappointed that seat is taken,
and I soften again.

As I stand up to speak You (#7), former friend,
pointedly get up and leave.
I say something endearing and everyone laughs,
and the idea for this poem starts to itch
—only one quick cookie on the way out—
and I'm my old self again.

I check my messages and see that
You (#8) have turned down my idea with such sincere regret
that I'd still work with you anytime, and
You (#9) have switched your party from the Saturday,
when I'm free, to the Sunday, when I'm not free, but

You (#10) have invited me to dinner on the Saturday.

During muted TV ads the poem sketches itself out
on the backs of old envelopes,
sparks an idea for a book.

Do I want to do all that work, I ask myself, or just be happy
in the still fresh company of all of you,
the bitter and the sweet,
like chocolate, which fuels, soothes, and uplifts us,

Better than chocolate, whose goal is heavenly,
You are what chocolate tries to be.

NOW

Bone's Business

The Femur Breaks *(Brandon, Manitoba)*

No one knows to take a photo just before
the pivotal moment:

Goodbyes after Thanksgiving dinner,
young family lingering at the door,
parents, boy with pet salamander, girl with doll,
my sister, the honorary grandmother
and me, her out-of-province guest.

Unseen behind me
the dog comes silently to join us
—take the photo now!—
black Lab, rose-coloured carpet
her sudden warmth against my ankle
startles.

I topple sideways,
flail for a vertical,
an orchid, but it passes by
in the instant arc of my fall,
soft dusk and fields beyond sheer curtains,
glittering fish in greenish tank,
child's open baseball mitt
—these fragments I now shore against my ruin—
onto the floor.

Bump wakes me. I see stars
through the back ambulance windows
—where's that Pisces constellation?—
rose-coloured streetlight as we turn the corner
cheering and sliding toward home plate.

Packing

My sister packs for my brief hospital stay:

My tablet and its charging cord,
a little device to make sure the cord doesn't break
and a heavy-duty extension cord that turns on and off:
these so I can access books and email;

two lined notebooks with my favourite high-end pencils,
new sharpener with an extra deep well;
these so I can write down more than meals and medications:

and, since I'm so far away from home,
her old robe perfectly folded, her old slippers;
she refuses to use my credit card to buy me new socks.

Bags stowed in the hospital cupboard, she sits at my bed,
recounts what's in each zippered pouch, each pocket:
toothbrush, tiny toiletries,
needles, small scissors, thread in various colours.
She lets me hold her hand; I avoid her arthritic thumb.

Outside the Operating Room
—I've fasted for twelve hours—
she plans the treats she'll bake me from our mother's recipes.

The surgical team in plastic bonnets one by one stop by,
saying their names and itemizing what they'll do to me.
She plans the meals for when I'm discharged to her home.

Right now my last words are
"Sedation, please, before the epidural."

....

It must be over: I'm lying there,
leg in the air. She's holding it up so she can wash it,
pats two dressings end to end over the long fresh scar,
slips me off the table back onto the bed,
packs me up in blankets for Recovery.

I keep calling her name, but she's so joyful,
she can't speak.

Dream

I dream a black and white cow
is sitting on a low branch of a tree.

My kind of cow, sitting there chewing,
happily going nowhere.
Its tail, however,
hangs down like a cat's and twitches.

The cat in me, tense tail extended,
prowls along the ground,
with sinuous purpose.

My monkey bounces off the sun,
the clouds, the rain,
the upper branches of the tree,

My tree, my branch,
my broken limb,

the limb I dreamt
was strong enough to hold a cow.

Accepting Metal

Accept living with metal;
accept living.

It's really the fractured bone's task now
to find a way to trust the metal plate,
held fast to it by seven screws
not to be bargained with.

It reels in this sudden arrangement
forged by pain,

But, tucked back safely in among the muscles,
incision firmly stapled shut and healing,
the bone accepts the metal's strength,
mistrusts its silence, can't decide,
a parallel privacy or forced embrace?

Nevertheless the bone fulfills its gradual business,
fusing into itself to bridge the spiral break
at the same time spontaneously fusing into the metal
—thus love grows—
as the metal's surface, too, creeps into the bone.

Outside, like a background score twice daily,
the beat of exercises rallies the surrounding muscles,
and so we live

Until one day the long-time-healing bone
is stronger than the metal;
they say that happens over time.

One day I'll walk again,
forget I never could,
forget what's now inside me,

and bone and metal co-exist,
companionable,
nothing more to say.

Fish Tank

Suppose, as I fell,
my head had hit the fish tank:

broken-off glass corner
deep in the side of my skull
familiar, like migraine

soothed by the slightly-warm
fish-temperature water
rivering onto the pale carpet
over the shards of glass and over me,

the water spilling carnivals of fish
to tumble over my thick blood
and flex themselves for freedom.
The spotted, striped, spectacularly-finned
—O, let me see their colours while I can—

fish off to find their ocean,
my ocean finding me.

In Rehab

Here we wear our clothes,
use wheelchairs;
the goal for now
to get ourselves to the dining room.

Facing each other all around the table,
what do we wish we could go back and do
without repercussions?

Drink and jay-walk.
Drive drowsily at night.
Ride a motorcycle, even a lighter one.
On horseback, move cattle.
Step off a curb in winter.
Step out of a bathtub.
Reach for a cup on the top shelf.
Stand quietly beside a dog.

Some of us go on to live in gentler places,
do none of those things.

One of us dies.

Meanwhile, in these quiet weeks
we face each other over meals
in thoughtfulness,

we who have waken to harsh light,
—heaven or hospital?—
grateful for how we got here
from the side of the road.

In the Night

A cruise must be like this, or a getaway vacation,
my stay in this small rehab hospital:
every pain attended to, home-cooked meals,
eleven new-met companions to play board games with.
Ceiling lights too bright? I wear my sun hat.

Then, to remind me why I'm here, a milestone,
a choice of sleeping positions: on my back, yes, but now
if I clutch the railing of the bed
I can sleep on my "good" side, too.

All that may have set the stage.

One morning they say I cried out in the night.
They touched my shoulder,
told me I was in hospital and everything was all right,
and I went back to sleep.
Strangeness to absorb.

Childhood exchanges came back to me:
"I'm not feeling well."
      "There's nothing wrong with you."
"I'm afraid"
      "There's nothing to be afraid of."

Best to live alone,
keep uncertainties close to the chest
or lace them with such complicated irony
that everyone laughs before the truth kicks in.

But here among afflicted others is a freedom:
safe to cry out in the night and be heard, let loose
the shock of my fall, my pain, my fear, embarrassment,
financial concerns for the near and distant future,
guilt—does my sister really want me so close by?

All these burst forth in that inarticulate cry.
Or did I utter words?
Was it one cry or two?
Did I call out to someone?

More precious than any answer
is the matter-of-fact response
—yes, patients sometimes do that—

which eased me, freed me from suspicion,
gave me casual comfort,
and I didn't even have to ask.

Watching the Olympics, 2018

Old, osteoporotic leg propped up
on the arm of my sister's sofa
to reduce the swelling—it really works—
as the fracture heals.

Not my choice to watch ice-dancing pairs;
the skaters twist and fly,
I twist my neck to see the screen,
that's one connection.

What am I in this picture? The flat acre of ice;
lying here wrapped in robes
I am already stiff and hoary.
Unsuspecting, have I traded youth for cold?

Though northern born I never learned to skate.
My sister tried to teach me, but I'm the elder
and unused to being helped. Then her friends tried,
merrily at my elbows in the winter sunshine,
an affectionate lark. I didn't understand
the laughter of their willingness—
skating was what you did with friends.

Instead, I've always sought out words, shapes, colours:
How satisfying Pyeong Chang is,
exotic spelling, possible pronunciations;
how fresh the kaleidoscope of skaters' names.

And the joined Olympic Rings,
their colours clear through the ice;
the changing flags, the crowds,
the skaters with and against each other
pair after pair; my dizzy gaze can hardly follow
their coloured costumes off the screen and back again.

A week or two and it's done.
That's better.
Out the window: silent prairie winter;
slowly, a bit more snow.

Zodiacs

In the Eastern zodiac I'm Horse, and proud of it.
I'm careful who I tell, though—
one broken leg and I'd be shot.

Here I am incognito as a human,
my 70-staple scar healing over a metal plate,
thigh pale and swollen like a fish.

Here in the West I'm Fish,
two Fish, that is, swimming in opposite directions:
one can always get away, no need for legs.
I could swim if someone drove me to an ocean
and removed my staples first.

Mid-continent-trapped in winter,
I am a grumbling creature with two legs,
one struggling at the moment.
I manage with a walker, room to room.
Cursing, meticulous,
I plod through my physio program, drop and rest, decide that
Plodding is not the kind of Horse I want to be.

Exercise is hope: each repetition, flexing of the rump
and I'm one iota stronger and more graceful,
tiny as those particular iotas may be.

The day is coming: Doctors will bring cake
and announce my leg is strong enough. I've done it!

Strong enough for what?
I'll fluff my mane and race around the Earth,
stirring up oceans, hoofing the tops of mountains,
leaping at last into the stars
so everyone will know how brave I've been!

Or maybe not: what is it to be human?
I can talk, read, write and make things.
I'll likely let my rocking chair embrace me,
take my time considering choices
as the stars wheel by.

The Missing Masculine

I think back to that pleasant hospital room—
four beds: three men and me—
that's how it's done now.

Returning there from surgery was a double waking,
as were mornings: all of us sponge-bathing in bed—
beds, plural, that is—
behind peach-coloured privacy curtains
but reflected in the windows of dark prairie winter.

A nice variety of men, but none of them you
back in our home city,

Now in my sister's pristine house,
a different kind of comfort.
Phone calls are easier
for longish chats with friends,
brief chats with you—nothing much to say,
my different kind of friend,
so far from touching.

Here as the white snow freshens itself all winter,
indoor boredom of exercises two hours daily
build toward a distant dream of flying home,
of meeting spring through my own high-rise window.

A double springtime it will be,
me standing tall at last in sunshine,
you standing taller there, enfolding me.

Birthday

Altitude should accompany rising age,
it seems. There is an upward stretching:
surely the meaning of our lives enlightens.

Remember the childhood expectation
as we grew taller every year, our hems let down,
or, with luck, new clothes; then out to play.

No thought then of the immanent arc ahead:
at full grown height a few years' arrogant driving,
then the slowly thickening responsibility called prime.

In time our spines diminish, making us shorter,
we grow heavier with accomplishments as if for ballast,
our steps weighty with meaning.

At the same time there is a lightening:
hair thins out, its colour leaves us,
though we can mask this fading;
small bones crumble from within,
marrow seeps from our longer bones unnoticed
till a fracture fells us for a bitter horizontal while,
leaving us fearful ever after.

Still, there is something rising,
as if our outgrown birthday candles
stacked themselves end to end
in one long flimsy column,
precarious as we ourselves become.

On top, the flickering prize:
the wits intact,
flame fed by rarefied air.

Saving the Monkey

Only the right word can save the monkey;
I'm the one to find it.

Others search also but the dream is clear:
I'm the one to save her.
While we work the monkey paces
—Do monkeys pace? Why not—
or maybe that's me limp-pacing in my urgency.

The word will name the one who feeds her,
hoses the ground around her
and to whom she extends her spindly arm
for injections.

The word suggests
a large man in a khaki shirt
who whistles his way toward her
with a bucket of carrots,
tosses them one by one for her to catch
—and there's the word: *zoo-keeper!*

She lets him call it playing.
She pretends this is a zoo with other monkeys,
pretends she is kept
till the man locks up and leaves.

Then is the monkey saved for soaring:
no creeping age
nor twinge of healing limb can hold her,
nor fiction of a cage confound her purpose.

I like that other word, *save:*
means keep,
means release.

Wheeling

Four-wheeled walker,
FWW,
not quite a curse word.

Cumbersome, deluxe, necessary—
which is the least forgivable?

Call it Secretariat,
Call it a flying machine:
words are not powerful enough.

Here I am trudging out in public, preceded
by this bright-blue-framed appendage.

Some people fear I'm in pain.
If they look at me they'll be implicated:
if they speak to me
they'll have to help me get a taxi
and be late for their appointment.

Some fear I'm afflicted
with a ghastly and permanent condition;
if I die on the spot
they'll have to call Emergency
and be late for their appointment,

One man speaks to me, asks
how to meet able-bodied women.

I keep moving.
The walker my companion
in the library, the supermarket;
I practice my improving gait along the aisles.
I say to everyone I pass
"It's just a broken leg. It doesn't hurt. It's healing well."

Perhaps I'm snarling, shouting;
in any case, nothing comes back
not even an echo.

Perhaps there was no real sound to begin with,
perhaps I'm just muttering
or, having thought those things
am calmer.

Walker-girded, I move smoothly now,
and faster.

Perhaps they see the walker,
shiny blue frame setting off the black,
leave space around me as they pass
or remember someone loved
and hold a door for me
or let me go ahead,

or warm to me as I enter an elevator
with you who also use a walker,
or you, child in a stroller.

I, who am about to rise, now greet you,
"Hey, everyone's got wheels!"
and the days start flowing.

Still Healing

Four wheels good, three legs better:
soon I'll be past the walker
onto a cane.

Then I'll be safely unremarkable among the many
cane-carrying members of society
with my shiny new Black Beauty,
bandanna knotted at its ferule
so no one claims it by mistake.

I'll be able to get into a house for a visit,
go to restaurants with lower-level washrooms,
get onto a stage to accept an award.

Two legs even better:
one day I'll just forget the cane and keep on walking.

And why stop there, with the femur?
My body, high on healing,
could grow other parts,
wings, for example—good thing I'm in control.

Yes, wings would help me
run upstairs two at a time,
or learn to ride a bike—why not?

Then I'd relax,
see where wings take me.

Leave-taking

The flight is booked, the airport help arranged.
I've agreed to travel with both cane and walker,
compromise with my sister
after our winter in her home.

This time we pack together, my large suitcase.
All I want to take home from our shared adventure,
her old dark paisley T-shirt I've adopted
and the four sandwich plates I bought
so we wouldn't keep running out of them.

Mobility, clothing, food—all bases covered.
Now we discuss at length
why I won't try to make room in the suitcase
for the jigsaw puzzle we never got to,
though I agree a package of sewing needles will fit.

Better that tiny spat than mentioning
the unanticipated:
paint chipped where the walker "kissed" the walls,
ruts worn across her year-old carpets
(good quality, the fibres will spring back).

The furniture she moved to clear a path for me,
will she put it back in place and then forget me?

Will the vests I've crocheted for her,
the blanket we've knitted jointly,
muffle any unspoken quarrels,

soften that I've left,
maintain the fitful, loving dream
that I was here at all?

Bones' Full Business

When you gallantly extend your hand to me
(I'm home, no longer need that kind of help),
the gesture fulfills
our months of stilted phone calls,
emails inadequate to our true connection.

When you extend your hand to me in invitation,
fingers near touching,
Michelangelo's great painting comes to mind,
those reaching, robust limbs,
God gently giving life to Adam
(it doesn't matter which is which,
we're all reclining).

It's our bones that bear us closer,
brace and release us into each other's warmth;
surely this is the bones' full business.

What good is talk unless we also
feel each other's rise and fall of breath?
And what good breath without familiar touch,
or touch, unless we move,
and move toward dance?

No one thinks of the bones implied
inside those faraway painted limbs, bearers of life.
Our bones, too, claim privacy,
hidden, ready for business,
inside our waking limbs where they belong.

The Octave Difference in Our Voices

Hat, October

He arrives one sunny afternoon in a new fedora
hangs it on the ladder-back chair,

red windbreaker on the chair, as well,
wide yellow tie,
new, balloon-patterned briefs,
worn-through socks,
sneakers neatly below.

He steps away and the chair, hung festive,
twirls round the room past the window
through the slanting sunlight,

twisting with its shadow in a *pas de deux*,
italic shadow that would write us down
or, if the chair stood still, would stretch us angular
and sketch us through the sunlight
onto the wooden floor.

Evening emerging from a softer place,
he forgets the colour of his hat
—it's new, after all—
but whistles as he strides as of on stilts to find it.

Selves

> *...only God, my dear,*
> *Could love you for yourself alone*
> *And not your yellow hair.*
>   —W.B. Yeats

What God-tempting features have we here?
Not hair: you're bald.
I like your classic look—grey fringe,
no danger of the latest hairstyle;
still, you grieve the loss of the thick and dark.

Must be your limbs, a gleam in God's eye
and in mine as I behold you:
limbs so long, and face, and torso too
seem even longer in their slenderness.
I ask small favours just to watch you move,
and as we lie together murmuring self to self
I sometimes sideways peek to try
to focus on your toes.

Our selves, our features, we are all akin—
you, I and Yeats's lovely friend:

Canaries, too, are yellow,
their selves sing to the shaft of sun
He's angled through their cage.
Giraffes, too, are long-limbed;
their selves, uniquely necked, reach for the crunch
and succulence of leafy twigs He's fashioned.

Here's my own self, blessed with a plethora of words
and the urge to use them,
and yours, my quiet, smooth-headed lover,
blushing as I read this to you.

Surely from His cold heaven

He sees, He hears, He loves
these selves He's made
and, surely with delight, adorned so.

Risen

Laboriously risen from the sea,
opposable thumbed,
we've come to this:
devices strewn on the bed

My new bed with its own remote:
thumb-clicks slowly raise the top or bottom
suggesting whims of comfort to the aged
        perhaps new bamboo sheets?

A remote for the TV:
one click and the world invades the bedroom
one more click to the parts I like
        gardens, giraffes

And the wireless phone
        how is that possible:
so mobile, friendly?

You ring from the downstairs lobby.
There you are, caught on the TV screen
        jacket already opened.
I buzz you in and banish the devices.

For us the bed is set at flat.
Naked as our forebears, faded,
in a slow tumble,
        breath, hair, saltiness of sweat
we re-enact begetting.

lie back in the after-warmth and rest
and talk. Remembering the remotes I offer
sitting up, watching TV:
        some comedy, some crime?

A larger choice awaits us.
We lie silent,
        lest we quarrel,

clinging to indecision,
for there is no answer:

Succumb to our devices,
         how they shape us,
or once again embrace,

Which is the talisman
against the long fall back?

Singing

You're on your way to me:
they won't keep still,
those special words we've uttered,
blooming into song.

Not your arriving words
—car park, stock market—
all those consonants soon go
the way of clothing

as we slow
into our smooth and hairy warmth,
wellspring of our being-here words,
song-like themselves

until our kisses mute them into mumbles,
into secret sounds that hover and keep safe
our long, shared leisure and our sleep.

The same words wake,
we speak them as we part.
Well, sad songs are okay:
sometimes you're here
and sometimes you're away.

Sunday Morning

Snow-roofed houses, dawn-still trees,
seen from my twelfth-floor window;
the only coloured thing, the traffic light.

Joggers outrun its winking changes,
claim the road—sidewalks not cleared—
ravenous for distance.

Dogs don't look up, dog walkers do,
on their stop-and-start way;
red light? just turn the corner.

A few cars wobble to the crossing,
drivers still waking grateful for order
as they hesitate.

Green light excites, cars go.
Where shall I go? How about—
light changes.

Once I would have called it yellow
but learned amber,
subtler, caution against haste.

Red light predictable
as flannel nightgowns,
same high-fibre breakfast.

Sunday morning:
a man and a woman are one,
a woman and a traffic light are one.

Potatoes

A startling gift: potatoes.
A ten-pound bag of potatoes
in my one-person kitchen.
You're going to cook them,
soothe my aging stomach.

Potatoes: no mellifluous name
nor graceful shape nor fetching colour;
colour subtle as the earth,
that's something.

No musical romance of pasta
nor widespread dignity of rice;
plainness straight from the earth,
land of our birth,
that's something.

You select two, and side by side we work.
I sort of rinse them;
water brightens the brown,
makes visible a network pattern, rootlets
or tiny fissures opening for growth.

You, no nonsense,
scrub till you wear off the peel, reveal
the colour of my skin,
networks of grey thatch define your shins.

Microwave allows six minutes
for a still embrace, another two
while the potatoes cool
till you retrieve them.

Small table, water glasses clink,
toes touch, yogurt is passed,
and yes,
the potato you have tamed to softness

after all does soothe my stomach,
gentle aftertaste of earth.

Not Seen nor Heard

Could we not see nor hear
the air would still connect us,
proof there is air

Proof of what they call
pheromones or pheronomes,
nuisance to remember

Whiffs of you beckon me,
small pungencies,
who said nectar was sweet?

Gamut of temperatures
entices touch to warm parts,
cool parts, warm parts

Slowness, too, is our friend:
let time cavort with air, abstract
but our own waves stir

Large movements animate the air,
the whiffs go wild awhile,
then welcome sweaty rest

Dozing I cool against your chest,
breath swells within your chest,
hair tickles,

Tickle sneezes, flails for a tissue,
back to blessed rest so close
no air between

Your heart beats strong,
mine fibrillates along,
not heard nor seen.

High-Rise Living, Two Afternoons

Once when we newly lay together here
in the thin-ribbed pattern of the sun
forced past the closed slats of the blind
we heard a thump, the window washer's feet
as he rappelled from floor to floor,
and while his shadow deftly worked
the squeegee in five minutes flat
we worked to force our whispered giggles still.

Now we are accustomed.
Don't take off your clothes quite yet,
I needn't warn you as you see, then smell
my newly-painted door propped open to dry.
We hear the painters knock and chat
to all the neighbours further down the hall
while, clad and separate,
with this this silent hour between us
we gently wait, look out the window.

Late Afternoon, My Place

Back from my moment in the bathroom,
back to you, stretched out in silent splendor on the bed,
I lie against your warmth and fall asleep.

When we were new, I would apologize.
Now, when I wake,
I reach up to your ear, and whisper, "TV?"
      "Sure."
It is so pleasant here against your ear
I ask once more, "TV? You're sure?"
      "Sure."

I can tell you like my whispering.
"You're really sure about TV, now?"
      "Okay."
I reach for the remote and fall asleep against your arm.

Waking, I find our favourite show.
I'd like to watch it,
I'd like better, ads muted, to listen to you talk about it,
      talk of many things,
But better still, lying here against your arm, your leg,
I fall asleep again.

Wordlessly we know it's time. Looking for your socks
how gracefully you bend over the side of the bed,
warm back to me,
where, with my cheek against you,
I could also sleep.

Your gifts to me
the luxury of touching, clinging, lingering
and this sleep which pulls me toward you,
pulls me deeper into me.

Old Cotton Robe

We could take off our clothes, I said ten years ago.
I offered you this favourite old robe of mine,
a dark blue geometric patterned cotton,
and chose for myself a flowered silky one.

I'd sewn the blue one from a printed sheet, the border
neat with binding down the front and on the pocket,
wore it on and off for thirty years before I offered it—
full length on me, knee length on you
and wrapped more copiously round your leanness.

I almost wore it out, those thirty years,
and it's survived another ten with you,
the doubled seams still holding well, still dark,
the rest all faded, threadbare and about to tear.

I say I'd make you a new one if I could
(surprised, *Old is okay*, you say)
but the age-related changes in my thumb
dissuade me from my trusty sewing machine.

Laundry day: behind my bedroom door it hangs
as you have left it, like a signature:
inside out, lopsided, right sleeve scrunched.

The robe holds us embraced:
my upward reach to its hook to take it down,
your recent scent that dwells there,
your voice that said *Old is okay,*
my tingling ear that heard it.

Early March Birthday

> *Sugar and spice and all things nice,*
> *that's what little girls are made of.*

Month of mud and promise
which will I wake to on my day—
grey rain cliché
or sunshine vanquishing new snow?

What cake-filled pigtailed eight-year-old
skipping at last on the open sidewalk
ever imagines 78?

What 77-year-old, seeing herself
in the jaunty slimness of those sevens
dares to imagine 78?

Now is the plumpness of my new-found eight,
sugar and spice like any other creed
taking its vengeance

In the East eight means prosperity
a little late for me, but look!
This poem, new as a robin,
agitates the branches of my mind,
with each day's editing the sun stays longer.

Eight on its side denotes infinity,
the symbol curling back but the sense,
straight line of time on its unrelenting path
one muddy day will simply drop me.

Meanwhile,
and a lovely while it is,
you hold me
call me sweet
and in the same tone
call me little.

Elder Sleepover

Why didn't we think of this before?
Our languorous afternoon, of course,
but then?

You come prepared:
your own water filter,
your goat weed tea,
your steel cut oats;
peaches and chocolate for me.

Why didn't we think of this before?
My evenings:
pink pill from the foil pack before dinner,
don't lie down for two hours,
two different pills with a glass of water,
don't lie down for another half hour.
Ten o'clock:
hearing aids out, bite guard in, thumb brace on.

And here you are, jaw trussed up
in your pale blue anti-snoring gear;
shy as strangers we sleep side by side.

I wake, as I sometimes do.
I could breathe deep to fall asleep again
or, grinning that you're here beside me,
tease this visit into a poem.

Can it be you hear me thinking?
A muffled syllable from you, murmur from me
and O, the thrill
of the octave difference in our voices in the dark,
our reaching hands!

Dedications

- "A Lesson in Resuscitation" is in memory of Hedy Hill
- "The Day She Never Saw the Weather" is in memory of Jan
- "Scattering" is in memory of Carol McGirr
- "Work" is for Patricia S. Johnston
- "January, Green" and "Sky Blue Umbrellas" are for Norma Rowen

- The poems in *Bone's Business* are for my sister, who invited me into her home for the long months of my recovery.

- The poems in *The Octave Difference in our Voices* are for LKB.

Acknowledgements

For moral support or practical advice or critical attention to my writing or eager requests to hear my poems during the adventure of this book, I thank:
- Allan Briesmaster, Heather Cadsby, Linda Nance Gibson, Maureen Scott Harris, Don McCloud, Norma Rowen, Kathleen Walton Smith;
- the ExEds: Ann Birch, Anne Denoon, Mary Frances Coady;
- the CALMers: Carol Enns, Allan Jenoff, Louise O'Neill;
- the Vic Poets;
- the warm, scintillating community that is the Arts & Letters Club of Toronto;
- and my publisher, Candice James, who turned my manuscript into a book, with promptness and patience.

Some poems in *Climbing the Rain* have appeared as follows:

Anthologies

- "It's There" forthcoming in *Hologram for P.K. Page,* ed. Yvonne Blomer and D.C.Reid
- "You x 10" in *Community,* Gertrude's Writing Room, spring 2022
- "Amethyst" in *101 Portraits,* Sandcrab Books, spring 2022
- "Late Afternoon, My Place" in *Love,* Volume 4 (October 2021) and "Work," titled "Returning," in *Work,* Volume 5 (February 2022) of the 12-volume *Lifespan* series, Pure Slush Press, Adelaide, Australia.
- "Flying Into Vancouver" in *Heartwood: Poems for the Love of Trees,* League of Canadian Poets, 2018)
- "Dinosaur Aloft" in *Seek It: Writers and Artists Do Sleep,* Red Claw Press, 2012).
- "A Lesson in Resuscitation" in *Tales for an Unknown City: Stories from One Thousand and One Friday Nights of Storytelling,* McGill-Queens University Press, 1990
- "The Goose and the Commuter Train" in *The Third Taboo, a Collection of Poems on Jealousy,* Wolsak and Wynn Publishers, 1983
- "Miracle near U. of T." in *Tributaries, an Anthology: Writer to Writer,* Mosaic Press, 1978
- "From Southern Ontario, a Sea Tale" in *Whale Sound,* Douglas and McIntyre, 1977

Journals

- "A is for," "October 2020, Walk to the Park," "Risen," "Sky Blue Umbrellas" and "Song without Nouns" in *Sage-ing: The Journal of Creative Aging*, September 2021
- "January 2021, Atonement" online in *Thunder Under the Mountain: Pandemic Poems* Volume IX, Issue III, Subterranean Blue Poetry, March 2021
- "From Southern Ontario, a Sea Tale" online on *Poetry Present,* 2020
- "It Wishes" online in *Tuesday Poems,* Ottawa, 2019
- "Summer Story, Yonge and Eglinton" and "The Day She Never Saw the Weather online in *Monday Poems*, Leaf Press, 2014
- "Dinosaur Aloft" in *Monday Poems*, Leaf Press, 2013
    also online in *Poetry Pause*, The League of Canadian Poets Poetry Pause March 2021

Author Profile

Marvyne Jenoff was born in Winnipeg and began publishing poems in Canadian literary journals as a student at the University of Manitoba in the 1960s.

Now a long-time resident of the Toronto area, she has published four books of poetry and short fiction with Canadian literary presses. Her poetry has appeared in anthologies and journal, both print and online, across Canada and internationally.

She is the subject of a video, which includes an interview and reading, in Kathleen Walton Smith's Creativity Interviews. Recorded in July 2021, the video is posted on the Mensa Canada Youtube Channel, accessible to the general public.

Marvyne Jenoff is a member of the League of Canadian Poets and The Writers Union of Canada. She is also a visual artist. For further information visit her website: www.marvynejenoff.org

www.ingramcontent.com/pod-product-compliance
Lightning Source LLC
Chambersburg PA
CBHW070914080526
44589CB00013B/1288